# Beautiful Escape

Cassie Lansdell

JASCAS PRESS

eISBN 978-0-9957391-0-9
Print ISBN 978-0-9957391-1-6

Cover photo by Nathan Cowley from Pexels.com

JASCAS PRESS
1796 Davenport House
261 Bolton Road
Bury
BL8 2NZ
jascaspress@outlook.com

# Contents

One more day  1

Black  2

Upon these streets  4

Until it's light  6

Beautiful escape  8

Body  10

Two minds  11

Four-letter word  12

Blind creator  15

Demon  16

Replace you  18

The pain is contagious  20

The mask  21

Forever high  22

In the sticks  24

Summer's not forever  26

Mrs Jane  28

Simply divine  29

Oh boy  30

Poser  31

Rewind the day  32

Poison gun  34

Revelation  36

Just let me love you  38

The sweetest thing  40

Basic life  42

About the author  44

## One more day

Took my medicine
Ready steady, here goes the torture
Take a deep breath
Step by step, welcome my new name
Spot my target
Now it's time to taste the poison
Break out my whip
Make it quick
Keep it locked in the brain

Make joy for them
There's a light at the end of the tunnel
Toy with them
Forget about today
You can escape tomorrow

What will be will be
Shining star in the sky, that's me
The light will come, I'll be free
One more day is all I see

## Black

If our time came
        Do you think our eyes would look the same?
Would you see me clear?
Could I trigger something in your brain?
That's been lost, all the years passed
You haven't seen my face
I wonder if you'd notice
All that's changed

If a time bomb was to land
        Would you take my hand?
Erase the past
Take back all the bad
Pull me away from black

Half of me's gone
Running through life trying to remain strong
If you knew the truth would you right your wrongs?
Let me see what I've dreamed
Not what I'm hiding from
If you could see what I am
Would you join me today?

Am I stupid to think you'd change?
Is this all one sided
Have we always been on the same page?
So many answers I'll never know
Should I fight?
Or realise there's nowhere for us to go?

## Upon these streets

Feathers, float around this scene
Chasing everything peacefully
Silence, beneath the rainbow tree
Here in this moment of clarity
Acceptance, whoever we may be
Take a dive in the sacred sea
Illusion, the same time every week
My brothers and sisters come to me

So what?
So what if our mouths don't speak?
They'll open to a certain degree
To pop another T
Taste on the tongue so sweet
So what?
So what if our bodies burn?
We're too critically insane to learn
No cause for concern
Tonight our prayers are heard

Let's dance around the fire
Pleasure upon these streets

Feathers, simple as they seem
Carry an air of mystery
People, all our complexities
Vanish as quick as a summer breeze
Four walls, the room in which we see
Open to allow our spirits free
Lonely, lonely as we've been
Feel somewhat of a dying breed

## Until it's light

He's far too sweet, like chocolate
That smell compelling my nose
And oh, it knows
Skin so soft, like the clouds in my sky
Floating until we take flight, it's our night
His eyes so bright, so pearly
Shine to awaken my eyes
Full of surprise
That touch around my body
So mesmerising

Oh, I'm falling hard again
Think I may love you till the end
This could be starting all over again
Can we stay friends?

You're my wicked friend
Tell the rest they can wait, you're my saviour
The one for me
You're mine
Until it's light

He's far too cool
Fear makes me feel so alive

Never shy
Taste so good, my creamy delight
You always get it right
He knows just how to please me
It doesn't stop, we're up all night
His rush it numbs my aching
Disguises me with his lies
Then I feel fine

Promise me, I'll promise you
We'll stick together like glue
Please me, I'll take care of you
Feels right just us two

## Beautiful escape

I'm stumbling down the road
I'm talking to the dead
I'm listening to the trees
Think I've done it again
I'm downing empty drinks
I'm zoning out the stares
It's time to take a seat
'Cause I've just done it again

I'm going down
My head's spinning round
Floating on a cloud
And I'm not coming back now

It's the same shit different day
        Yes, OK, I'll grow up now
You'll throw your life away
        Yes, I know, but I'm stuck in this haze

A beautiful escape

It starts at 10 pm
We rock up to the place
The bass is hot

You feel the rush
And I'm going to cave
A few looks around the room
That smile on every face
I'm with the crowd
The time is now
I'm about to cave

I'm going down
My head's spinning round
Floating on a cloud
And I'm not coming back now

That look in your eye is telling me it's not enough
Now to my own surprise
I'm falling into a beautiful escape

Skies of pink
Your glitter shines so bright
Now honey and seas of gold
It's gone cold and I'm drowning anyway

## Body

Our colours combining to break through
So intertwined, me and you
A spiritual guidance we can't move
Oh look at, just look at the view

I'm with your body
Feel my body
Come and take me into your world
We won't stop flying
I'll be your fantasy girl

I'll go down, my love
Synchronising touch
Make me what you want
Intensity from above

There is no one but you I'd scream for
Not intoxication, it's much more
The magic you fill me with, I adore
I lose all control when I fall

## Two minds

Their visions emulate exquisite designs
Their apprehensions inhumed once again
An optical illusion in two minds
One more recipe for disaster
To add to their hidden treasure chest

Why does history repeat itself?
A question that will forever linger on their lips
Are we human? Have we crucified ourselves?
Thoughts they are yet to ponder
Instead they speak of hell
To get their kicks

## Four-letter word

I blur out the red noise
To get by
The screams turn to echoes
One last try
To run from this black hole
And get away

But you won't escape my mind
I tell you to leave me
Then I cry

You hold me so close
And now I
Can't break from this bad dream
Don't know why
It's the same thing every time

We're on this mad trip
Up and down
Let me go
Wrapped in your arms
So I don't hit the ground
Now I'm stuck
In this four-letter word

We've been here a year now
Who'd have known
Your ten thousand sorrys
Wouldn't show
It's time to say goodbye

But there's hope
And I keep walking down this road

A part of me hates you
When you show that you can't contain it
You just blow into something crazy
I should go
But I can't let go of this rope

Take me to that place I know
Drag me in, don't let me out
It's time to walk this world alone
Don't let me sink, don't let me drown

I'm burning up
No time to run and hide
Back to all I know
It's time to grow

So I'm not
Stuck in this four-letter word
Love

I love you

# Blind creator

Sink in my big fat red cushion
A place where angels sing
God bless my heroine
Pretty little thing
Fly me to a vivid galaxy
Palpitations, just breathe
No more calamity
Psychedelic D

Call me the chronovator
Forget the devil chaser
Call me the revelatory
Here in my hidden chamber

I'll be a blind creator

Float into the sky
Elevate my mind
Reaching for the everlasting high
Here in this moment
Feeling so alive
My friend and I

# Demon

Cut the chain
It's been broken again
Trap doors are always closing
Blow your troubles away
Just wish you had it in you one day
Signal that brain
Tear it into little pieces
Complete the puzzle

Make it rain
Let it pour
The demon in your mind
Will never cross those walls
Face the pain
Pull through the fall
You'll thank your body later
For every day more

Look, your hands are frozen
Choking up with the flames that have spoken
Covered with stars aligned to hide the dark in
          your heart
Twelve years riding on from the start

Lay those shakes to rest
Find a bit of air in that chest
Put it to bed
Find the will you've been searching for instead

## Replace you

Can we pretend, darling
That you know my name?
Why don't you stop
All these pathetic games?
No need to ask why
You always play
Afraid of hurt
Scared of change

You can't always run
It gets harder
Take this chance, lover

Don't act like you're no good
'Cause you think you should
I'll just replace you

One step forward
Then five steps back all the time
Stop all the confusion in my mind
Is this the real you?
Can you decide?
I'm done allowing players into my life

Never forget what it's like
When you get turned down
Like you're not worth anything
You do it to me
I just want you to see
That I will never let this happen again

You can't always run
It will get harder
So take this chance, lover

## The pain is contagious

How can I prepare
For an earthquake to flare up
Knock me into some kind of twisted pleasure state?
Was this my fate?

Why do you eat me up?
Yet you complete me, my love
A poisoned chalice sent from above
My heavenly cry
My most fatal high

But the pain is contagious
Living to be dangerous
Or am I living to be shameless?

He's locked me in
With his tainted angel wings
And he wants to play
But this time round my skills are rusty
I'm leading with my heart
Now it's led me astray

## The mask

My actions allow me to deceive
Sell my soul, bare it all
My constant fallacies lead me to believe
Sell my soul, the curtain calls

The mask is no longer a mask
No beaming light illuminates the dark
It was I, the chosen one
I chose with my heart
However soon it all ends
I will become the part

# Forever high

It was Wednesday, the night we met
You thought I'd forget, you knew I was bent
Heading more and more west
You were persistent, so I said yes
I let you know it would be something to regret
The more deep we get

I told you, don't fall for me
Don't ever fall for me
I am the biggest risk
A mess covered in bliss
Why did you unleash me
The devil that lives in me?
You are my biggest hit
One I cannot quit

I'll never cry
Too many endless nights
Sorry babe, I try
Just forever high

It was Friday, the night you left
A night I can't forget, fucked up in every sense
Feeling more and more dead

You were adamant it was the end
But I did say this was dangerous, my friend
Now the more and more we can't pretend

## In the sticks

You can't take the nitty gritty or the city out the
        kiddy
But let them ride
Experiencing alternative places
Residing in a new life
So let the tumbleweeds fly
Over a crazy land
Where the heat's so dry
All the flies, buzzing around your eyes
No worries, we got our disguise
Walking through the never-ending vines

It's cool, man
We've got this
We're out here in this ruckus
These days we'll reminisce
Three months of madness
In the sticks

You won't take the nitty gritty or the city out the
        kiddy
But let them ride
Experiencing alternative faces
Drinking all the whisky and the wine

Chilling beneath the stars
Pass me the French fries
We stand by, huddled around the fire
No dramas till midnight strikes
Tearing up the peaceful delight

## Summer's not forever

Days lost, again
Spending almost every single night away from my bed
Oh, when will this end
This life's become a harsh reality

No more can I pretend
That summer's not forever
It's time for me to change
But why can I not seem to let go?
Just want to go back to that place
Runs deep in my veins
Kiss the old me away

You've got me hanging on this tightrope
And I can't keep hanging on this tightrope
If I fall will you catch me?

No light where I am
Paranoia strikes and all the heavy thoughts rush to my
        head
Fun's over, what's left?
Fear, loneliness and deep regret
Now that dream's a mess

Summer's not forever
That carefree life will never change
It's easy to forget the real world
But nothing ever stays the same
Kiss the old me away

## Mrs Jane

Bombs away, short-lived delay
Momentary burning, magical flames
One more you say, sure if I may
My kryptonite, oh Mrs Jane, Mrs Jane

Don't ever fade, never Jane
Here's where we'll lay, Mrs Jane
Let's waste the day, Mrs Jane
Oh Mrs Jane, Mary Jane

Never leave, never leave
Keep me free, stay with me

Bombs away, smouldering gaze
Visual beauty, top of the grades
Taste the rain, my sugar cane
My Kryptonite, oh Mrs Jane, Mrs Jane

My choochoo train, Mrs Jane
Conceal the pain, Mrs Jane
Let's play all day, Mrs Jane
Oh Mrs Jane, Mary Jane

Never leave, never leave
Keep me free, stay with me

## Simply divine

Come and awaken
Come and revive
Come be my ocean nymph
Come and redesign
Hold the shrine
Embark on life
Now it's time
And time is simply divine
The moon and the stars will align
This time it's simply divine

Come and surpass my goal
Come to me
We'll overflow in these liquid dreams
Let them shine
Drink the wine
Now it's time
And time is simply divine
My aura is clear in your eyes
Now time is simply divine
Our energy fields are rewired
This time it's simply divine

# Oh boy

There's plenty more to see than just white
Oh boy, why don't you take your mother out tonight?
Dance and laugh around the bar
Have a cheeky glass of the old man's finest
Reminisce about the past
There's no chance of dismay, not the slightest
You can rekindle the brightness

Oh don't let the downs be downs
Kings were men before the crown
You'll always attract a crowd
And she'll always remain proud

So toast the night away
Toast to the love and hate
Just toast the night away
Here's to a greater day

There's plenty more to see than just brown
Oh boy, those smokes and pipes eventually burn out
Crack a smile, turn the page
Have another glass of the old man's finest
Pour your troubles down the drain
There's no chance of dismay, not the slightest
Who said you can't be united?

# Poser

Why don't you like me when I'm not sober?
Can I rest my head on your shoulder?
Sorry I'm not the girl next door
Come and pick me up off the floor

I'm a picture-perfect mess
How about you draw me instead?

You call me a boaster
But you're just a poser

Why do you hate me when I'm hungover?
Stop screwing and screw me on my four-poster
Sorry I'm not the perfect one
But you're just a joker

## Rewind the day

Take back my score
I rocked the boat
All to provoke a man who broke
Ignorant mind
How I betrayed, fell in the game
You never played

Let's rewind the day
Let's reverse the pain
I'll take your pain
I take it all back today

It was never you
What a cliché
But all the way
You gave and gave
What could have grown
Was overthrown
When I was shown to the unknown

Needed to go, needed to fall
Now years have passed
I know where to start

I show remorse for all I caused
I take it all back today

## Poison gun

Hold me for the last time
Then I'll say goodbye
Your chest will cover my chest
Allow me to hide

From all the mess that you threw up
Mess that's destroyed my mind
I'll escape from the mess that you blew up
Mess that's surrounded me
Just one more night

Now I feel so cold
Drinking into the unknown
Fill my bottomless holes
With the poison from this gun
Wrap it round my restless tongue
Drowning in love

Don't hold me any more
Hold her instead
Your debt will cover her debt
Heal a heart that's dead

Ignore the pain that's within you
Pain that will never compare
To every pain that's within me
Pain dripping through my veins
Now you don't have to care

# Revelation

Meet, meet my family
We, we fight in what we believe
He, he always lived to tell me
Our plans laid out under the tree
To set our people free
The power is me

Come alive
Open your eyes
Here's my surprise
Bleed

Revelation, book of revelation
Calling for his return
Knock that rocky road down
Elimination
They'll be sorry they stirred
She is coming down fast
Time to stand our ground
Look out

Meet, meet my family
We, drip in our sugar-cube dreams
He, he wants me to do his deed
No more time to practise peace
Prepare our rise above the heat
The power is me

My controls they break bones
One, two, three
Go nuts, take charge
My controls create red walls
Four, five, six, this world is ours

## Just let me love you

Although we don't come from the same world
I know, you know
You are meant just for me
Without you my body it feels cold
I know, you know
We can no longer dream
Baby if we keep the peace
Forever we'll be adored
I would rather risk it all
That's how hard you make me fall
Leave all your plans and let's run free
To a place we'll see the sun
You know, I know
It is time to see

Everyone seems sure about the answers
It's the world we live in, always critical
But time fades away when you come closer
When you see me, when you touch me
It was never planned, meeting each other
You were meant to stay away, that I'm sure
Every second hurts being without you
'Cause you love me
And I love you

Don't give up
I'm here waiting
Let's make history
Feel me now
Kiss me now
We won't stop
Their eyes bleeding
But we'll be living
Love me now
Touch me now
Just let me love you

Wrap my legs around you, move our bodies slow
We'll be up till morning, no control
Just let me love you

## The sweetest thing

I'm not here
You can't see me, dear
My best magic trick this year
A never-ending cheer
The one you used to know
Is now a headline show
Rip apart my soul
Not coming back home

Sweet, it's the sweetest thing
When the devil sings
Live on stage, it begins
Hanging by a string
Dangling

I, I, I always wanted to fly
Euphoria lives only up this high
And I will paint my future in time
Now broken wings won't shatter my mind

The world is grey
Every day
Taking endless photographs
Hanging on display
The stars disappear, go their separate ways
Laid out on the muddy grass
Letting dark light up the day

## Basic life

Can't hear the lingering sound
Two heads drifting in the clouds
A sea of champagne
Under a gridlocked plane
But our way's always the right way

Only hear screams from the crowd
The royals all take a bow
The world knows our name
Stumbling over the stage
Let's wish that basic life away

We're cruising
We're bruising
Illusion
Delusion

Welcome to our Shangri-La
Leave all your plans and get lost in the stars
We are living to die young
Playing safe has never won

Floating in and out of consciousness
We made our beds and swam through all the debt
I can only hear that bass line running in my mind
Waved bye to complications, hello to too many lines

A boom boom boom, come see the fresh hits in our
            room
Stacks on stacks, racks on racks, would make your
            dog sing woof woof
The greener the better, less of the worries, less of the
            grind
So take your negativity and shove it up your...
Let it shine

## ABOUT THE AUTHOR

Cassie Lansdell is a singer-songwriter and poet.
Born in London, she now lives in Sydney, Australia
with her boxer, Reggie.

www.ingramcontent.com/pod-product-compliance
Lightning Source LLC
Chambersburg PA
CBHW060542030426
42337CB00021B/4392